MATH ON
THE MOON

By Shalini Saxena

Gareth Stevens
PUBLISHING

Please visit our website, www.garethstevens.com. For a free color catalog of all our high-quality books, call toll free 1-800-542-2595 or fax 1-877-542-2596.

Library of Congress Cataloging-in-Publication Data

Names: Saxena, Shalini, 1982- author.
Title: Math on the moon / Shalini Saxena.
Description: New York : Gareth Stevens Publishing, [2017] | Series: Solve it!
  Math in space | Includes bibliographical references and index.
Identifiers: LCCN 2015051086 | ISBN 9781482449402 (pbk.) | ISBN 9781482449341 (library bound) | ISBN 9781482449242 (6 pack)
Subjects: LCSH: Moon–Juvenile literature. | Mathematics–Juvenile literature.
Classification: LCC QB582 .S29 2017 | DDC 523.3–dc23
LC record available at http://lccn.loc.gov/2015051086

First Edition

Published in 2017 by
Gareth Stevens Publishing
111 East 14th Street, Suite 349
New York, NY 10003

Copyright © 2017 Gareth Stevens Publishing

Designer: Laura Bowen
Editor: Therese Shea

Photo credits: Cover, p. 1 (moon) dzika_mrowka/Shutterstock.com; cover, p. 1 (metal banner) Eky Studio/Shutterstock.com; cover, pp. 1–24 (striped banner) M. Stasy/Shutterstock.com; cover, pp. 1–24 (stars) angelinast/Shutterstock.com; cover, pp. 1–24 (math pattern) Marina Sun/Shutterstock.com; pp. 4–24 (text box) Paper Street Design/Shutterstock.com; pp. 5, 17, 19 courtesy of NASA.com; p. 7 Aphelleon/Shutterstock.com; p. 9 Arnie Rosner/Photolibrary/Getty Images; p. 11 (top) Paul J Martin/Shutterstock.com; p. 11 (bottom) Desigua/Shutterstock.com; p. 13 Castleski/Shutterstock.com; p. 15 ASIF HASSAN/AFP/Getty Images; p. 21 Stocktrek Images/Getty Images.

Printed in the United States of America

CPSIA compliance information: Batch #CS16GS: For further information contact Gareth Stevens, New York, New York at 1-800-542-2595.

CONTENTS

Mission to the Moon 4

What Is the Moon? 6

Our Nearest Neighbor 8

The Moon's Pull 10

Phases of the Moon 12

Where Did the Moon Go? 14

No Cheese Here 16

Moon Walking 18

One Giant Leap 20

Glossary 22

For More Information 23

Index 24

Words in the glossary appear in **bold** type the first time they are used in the text.

MISSION TO THE MOON

People have long looked up at the night sky and wondered about our moon. Thanks to spacecraft and other special tools and machines, we now know it's an important part of our **solar system**.

In 1969, **astronauts** Neil Armstrong and Edwin "Buzz" Aldrin Jr. became the first people to walk on the moon. Since then, there have been other moon **missions**. In this book, you are the **lunar** explorer. How do you learn about something so far away? It's easier than you think! Ready for blastoff?

YOUR MISSION

You're already familiar with one tool of exploration. Math is one of the most important tools scientists use. In this book, your mission is to use math to solve some of the moon's many mysteries. Look for the upside-down answers to check your work.

The *Apollo 11* mission marked the first moon landing. After taking his first step on the moon, Neil Armstrong famously said: "That's one small step for [a] man, one giant leap for mankind."

5

WHAT IS THE MOON?

The moon might look like a planet, but it's actually a **satellite** that orbits, or goes around, Earth. It takes about 27 Earth days to make this complete trip. A planet orbits a star (like our sun), but a moon orbits a planet. Other planets have moons, too. Jupiter has 67!

YOUR MISSION

As it orbits Earth, the moon spins around. The amount of time it takes to finish 1 spin is equal to 1 moon day. That's about 656 hours, or more than 27 Earth days! About how many hours longer is a moon day than an Earth day?

$$656 - 24 = ?$$

Just as the moon orbits Earth, Earth orbits the sun. Because the sun is farther from Earth than the moon, the two appear to be a similar size to us. The sun is much larger, though.

ANSWER: A moon day is about 632 hours longer than an Earth day.

OUR NEAREST NEIGHBOR

The moon is an average distance of about 240,000 miles (386,240 km) from Earth. That may seem like a lot, but the moon is actually the space body closest to us. It's smaller than most planets, but we can see it so brightly at night because it's closer than any planet. Our moon is one of the larger moons in the solar system.

YOUR MISSION

A diameter is an imaginary line that runs from one side of a round object to the other through its center. The diameter of the moon is 2,159 miles, or 3,475 kilometers. Earth's diameter is 5,767 miles, or 9,281 kilometers, longer. Find Earth's diameter in miles and kilometers.

$$2{,}159 + 5{,}767 = ?$$ $$3{,}475 + 9{,}281 = ?$$

The moon is about 1/4 the size of Earth.

ANSWER: Earth's diameter is 7,926 miles, or 12,756 kilometers.

THE MOON'S PULL

The moon is close enough to Earth that its **gravity** causes bodies of water on Earth to rise and fall. Lunar gravity creates tides in our seas and oceans. When the moon's gravity pulls on one side of Earth, it causes the water to "bulge," or swell, in its direction. A bulge is also created on the opposite side of Earth. Earth is being pulled away from the water!

YOUR MISSION

Coastal areas on Earth have 2 high tides and 2 low tides every day. The time between 2 high tides is 12 hours and 25 minutes. The time between a high tide and a low tide is 1/2 of that. How much time passes between a high tide and the low tide that follows?

12 hours 25 minutes ÷ 2 = ?

The position of the sun also affects tides. When the moon and sun are lined up a certain way, they have a strong combined gravitational pull and cause very high or very low tides.

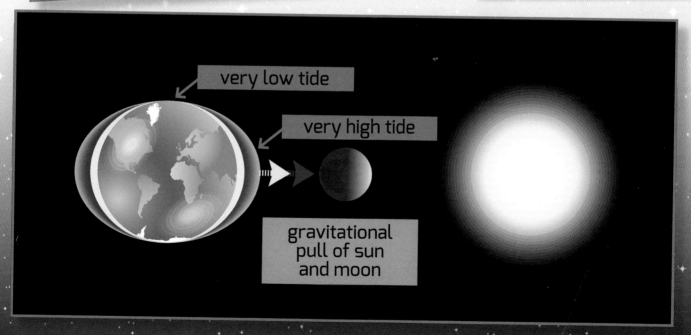

very low tide

very high tide

gravitational pull of sun and moon

ANSWER: The time between a high tide and a low tide is 6 hours and 12 1/2 minutes.

11

PHASES OF THE MOON

The moon has no light of its own. "Moonlight" is actually light from the sun **reflecting** off different amounts of the moon as the moon orbits. This means that sometimes the moon looks like a circle, and other times, it looks more like the letter C. In different **phases**, the moon seems to have different shapes, though it never actually changes.

YOUR MISSION

The following are the 8 lunar phases in order: 1) new moon, 2) waxing crescent, 3) first quarter, 4) waxing gibbous, 5) full moon, 6) waning gibbous, 7) last quarter, 8) waning crescent.

Beginning with a new moon, what fraction of the phases has passed before a full moon appears?

$$\frac{\text{phases that have passed before full moon}}{\text{all phases}} = \frac{?}{?}$$

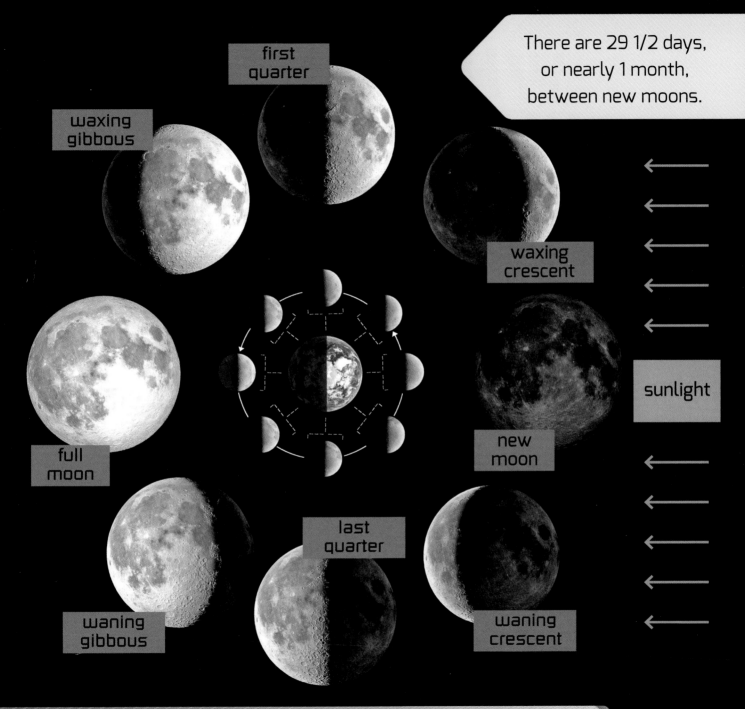

first quarter

waxing gibbous

There are 29 1/2 days, or nearly 1 month, between new moons.

waxing crescent

sunlight

new moon

full moon

last quarter

waning gibbous

waning crescent

ANSWER: Beginning with a new moon, 4/8, or 1/2, of the phases have passed before a full moon appears.

13

WHERE DID THE MOON GO?

Every so often, an event called a lunar eclipse makes it seem like the moon has disappeared. During a lunar eclipse, Earth passes between the sun and the moon and casts its shadow on the moon. Some lunar eclipses are total, which means the moon looks covered in darkness. In partial lunar eclipses, only part of the moon is covered.

YOUR MISSION

During a **penumbral** eclipse, Earth's outer shadow falls on the moon. Use the table on page 15 to find the difference in the number of penumbral and total eclipses occurring from 2017 to 2020. What fraction represents the number of penumbral eclipses in the table?

penumbral eclipses − total eclipses = ?

$$\frac{\text{penumbral eclipses}}{\text{all eclipses}} = \frac{?}{?}$$

14

LUNAR ECLIPSES, 2017–2020

February 11, 2017	penumbral
August 7, 2017	partial
January 31, 2018	total
July 27, 2018	total
January 21, 2019	total
July 16, 2019	partial
January 10, 2020	penumbral
June 5, 2020	penumbral
July 5, 2020	penumbral
November 30, 2020	penumbral

Part of the moon can be seen in the beginning of a total eclipse. But by the end, you'll see very little of it—or none at all.

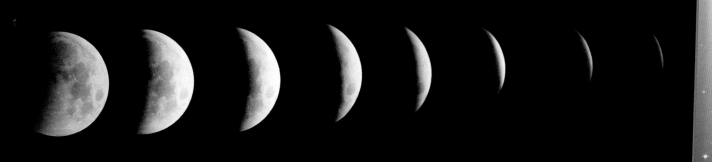

ANSWER: There are 2 more penumbral eclipses than total eclipses. In the table, 5/10, or 1/2, of the eclipses are penumbral.

NO CHEESE HERE

The bowl-shaped areas you might see in pictures of the moon are called craters. They're made by asteroids and **comets** that crashed there. These objects also created rocks and soil found on the surface. Some of the surface was formed by lava, or hot liquid rock, from **volcanic eruptions** billions of years ago.

YOUR MISSION

The highest point on Earth, Mount Everest, is 29,035 feet, or 8,850 meters, above sea level. The tallest point on the moon is 6,352 feet, or 1,936 meters, higher than this. What is the height of the highest point on the moon in feet and meters?

$$29,035 + 6,352 = ?$$ $$8,850 + 1,936 = ?$$

According to scientists, the rocks and soil found on the moon are similar to those on Earth. So far, they show no signs of life. The temperatures on the moon can range from −243°F (−153°C) to 253°F (123°C)!

ANSWER: The height of the highest point on the moon is 35,387 feet, or 10,786 meters.

MOON WALKING

Gravity is what keeps our feet on the ground. Walking on the moon would look funny to us because the moon's gravity is weaker than Earth's. Gravity also affects an object's weight. Weight is the measure of how much gravity pulls on an object's **mass**. Earth's gravity is 6 times stronger than the moon's, so an object's weight is 6 times more on Earth.

YOUR MISSION

If an object weighs 60 pounds on the moon, how much does it weigh on Earth? If an object weighs 60 pounds on Earth, how much does it weigh on the moon?

$$60 \times 6 = ? \qquad 60 \div 6 = ?$$

Because of the moon's weaker gravity, astronauts walking on the moon look like they're bouncing or floating.

ANSWER: An object that weighs 60 pounds on the moon weighs 360 pounds (163 kg) on Earth. An object that weighs 60 pounds on Earth weighs 10 pounds (4.5 kg) on the moon.

19

ONE GIANT LEAP

No one has walked on the moon since 1972, but satellites and other tools still send us facts about it. One spacecraft even discovered water. Manned missions to other parts of space might be able to use this water someday. Scientists can't wait to see what else they'll discover!

YOUR MISSION

Two people walked on the moon as part of *Apollo 11*. By February 1971, the number of people to walk on the moon tripled. How many people had walked on the moon by February 1971? The number of people who have walked on the moon in all is 2 times that answer. How many people have walked on the moon in all?

$$2 \times 3 = y \qquad y \times 2 = ?$$

In 2009, the *Lunar Crater Observation and Sensing Satellite* (LCROSS) proved that there's water under the surface of the moon.

ANSWER: By February 1971, 6 people had walked on the moon. In all, 12 people have walked on the moon.

GLOSSARY

astronaut: someone who works or lives in space

comet: a space object made of ice and dust that has a long glowing tail when it passes close to the sun

gravity: the force that pulls objects toward the center of a planet, moon, or star

lunar: having to do with the moon

mass: the amount of matter in an object

mission: a task or job a group must perform

penumbral: describing a space partly lit, between the shadow on all sides and the full light

phase: a stage in a process or chain of events

reflect: to throw back light, heat, or sound

satellite: an object that circles Earth. Man-made satellites collect and send information or aid in communication.

solar system: the sun and all the space objects that orbit it, including the planets and their moons

volcanic eruption: the bursting forth of hot, liquid rock from within a planet or moon

FOR MORE INFORMATION

Books

Close, Edward. *Moon Missions.* New York, NY: PowerKids Press, 2014.

Owen, Ruth. *The Moon.* New York, NY: Windmill Books, 2014.

Ross, Stewart. *Moon.* New York, NY: Scholastic, 2009.

Websites

Earth's Moon
solarsystem.nasa.gov/kids/index.cfm?Filename=moon_kids
Read more about our natural satellite—the moon.

The Moon
www.planetsforkids.org/moon-moon.html
See a detailed map of the moon and learn about its phases.

INDEX

Apollo 11 5, 20

Armstrong, Neil 4, 5

astronauts 4, 19

craters 16

diameter 8

eclipse 14, 15

gravity 10, 18, 19

highest point 16

LCROSS 21

light 12

phases 12

planet 6, 8

rocks 16, 17

soil 16, 17

solar system 4, 8

spacecraft 4, 20

sun 6, 7, 11, 12, 14

tides 10, 11

volcanic eruptions 16

water 10, 20, 21

weight 18